winter pruning

winter pruning

✧

wanda d. cook

STARK MOUNTAIN PRESS

winter pruning
Pocket Edition

Published by:
Stark Mountain Press
364 Wilson Hill Rd.
Colrain, MA 01340
starkmtpress@gmail.com

Stark Mountain Press website:
http://starkmountainpress.tripod.com/

Cover Design: Wanda D. Cook

ISBN: 978-0-9832298-8-9

With gratitude to

E. H. who encouraged me to step onto the path

and

L. K. who guided me along the way

Foreword

Our wait is over. She has been writing them for almost twenty years, and now we have a book of Wanda Cook's haiku. And not one of the broadsheets or mini-chapbooks — she has done those already, as well as editing two anthologies and co-editing a haiku anthology — but a real book of haiku. You'll find it was well worth the wait.

Winter Pruning is a solid collection, spanning the distances from a baby's curled fist to the distant stars and relating humanity to Nature at every turn. To demonstrate, I could point to one of my favorites in the book:

> so unconcerned
> with how i live
> this winter moon

Such a beautiful image so full of ambiguity.

There's a tantalizing handful of Wanda's justly famous erotic haiku here as well. Not many poets can write a haiku as delicate and sensual as:

> october afternoon
> the sighs of spent lovers
> or rustling leaves?

A certain wistful nostalgia pervades many of Wanda's poems, akin to driving through rural New England in Indian summer and stopping off at an antique shop. You might find a wooden spoon, an old milk can, a maple sugar bucket, or a child's sled.

Family is a frequent subject of Wanda's poems as she writes about her grandmother, parents, children and, of course, her own childhood, both in the city and on the farm.

Wanda writes from a solid grounding in the Japanese masters. I find flickers of Bashō in her haiku about children playing in the snow and her contemplation of the tidy grass at the grave of her father, who died young. Issa's love for the smaller creatures is here too, reincarnated in a struggling beetle, a tiny spider, a little hoppy toad, and a fledgling robin. Wanda can hear the voices of sunflowers, willow branches, and sea grass — and she translates them for us.

So don't tarry here any longer. Turn the page and get on with savoring these delicacies!

Charles Trumbull
Santa Fe, New Mexico

winter pruning

winter!
playing till the bite
of snow-crusted wrists

farm kitchen
the familiar scent
of drying mittens

morning fog
joining our gardens
the scent of lavender

first library card
taking in the scent
of unread books

    story hour
        the lean of first graders
            for the turn of the page

reading his journals
will I too
become so lonely?

prompting the fledgling
robin
&
i

noisy cardinal
are you excited
about dogwood blossoms too?

conversing
wilted sunflowers
in an old milk can

no longer able
to recall his voice
stilled willow branches

a hushed rustling
of winter sea grass
the secret she tells him

fiddlehead time
the tiny pink fist
of our firstborn

their sap bucket
on the wrong kind of maple
new neighbors

fog shift
the bare bones
of a november tree

what dreams?
the tidy grass
on my young father's grave

autumn gust
in the zen garden
nothing stirs

such stillness
a monarch
on her tiny finger

holding my breath
as the small bird feeds . . .
hands of st. francis

in the mid of night
wail of the loon
and your breathing

her sixth month
in the garden she selects
buds over blooms

budding season
lips pursed
for her first lipstick

tarpaper beach – *
her charcoal sketches
of apple blossoms

*the roof of an apartment or tenement building

crime scene
a ghetto child outlines
her doll in chalk

so unconcerned
with how i live
this winter moon

rustling autumn
the snip of scissors
on winter wool

tossed to the street vendor
the nanna's knotted blue hanky
*cinque**

cinque: (chin' - kwi)   Italian for five

midnight at the laundromat
washing clothes
in a red satin gown

louie, ella
and dinner by candlelight
dancing cheek to cheek

howling winter night
making love
with socks on

lantern light
that place on his back
where hollow meets curve

anniversary night
arranging her body
how it used to fit his

summer's end
instead of love songs crickets
from ruby's roadhouse

carrying the harvest
the rhythm
of her hips

st. joseph's feast day
he eyes up the girl
in the skimpy red dress

mother's eightieth
she toasts herself
with a bit of plum wine

again that same crow
another birthday
almost here

worlds in collision
i introduce
my two friends

but look –
this tiny spider and i
sharing the sun

this autumn
i pause to right
a struggling beetle

chipmunk –
just because i saved the beetle
don't assume i want you here

little hoppy toad
first human
of the season?

a final bulb
the warmth of garden soil
just after sunset

in his chubby hand
bent dandelions
. . . just three

king of the mountain
the tickle of dandelions
on the way down

grandchildren convinced
the museum sled was mine –
what can i say

fresh snow
the cat prints
change direction

his late season letter –
he risks
you're charming

a robin calls to its mate –
how many words
in a lifetime?

night of the supermoon
she begins a letter
to a distant friend

smoothing my journal page
green tea
in a white cup

on the front stoop shelling peas
one by one
grandma's stories

the pattern of gram's wooden spoon
on newly worked butter
starry night

a full moon
where branches once were
        winter pruning

breathing meditation
the nameless color
of the sky

the answers to why
no longer important
autumn equinox

gull or kite –
for the wind
what difference?

october afternoon
the sighs of spent lovers
or rustling leaves?

indian summer
the flicker
of minnows ~~~ our toes

winter night
in bed imaging him
. . . imagining it

2:00 a.m. thoughts
the sound of big

·

drop

·

rain

·

Publication Credits

Grateful acknowledgment is made to the editors of the following publications in which some of these poems appeared in present or earlier versions: Anita Sadler Weiss Competition (2007 HM); bottle rockets; dandelion clocks (HSA 2008 Anthology); Dasoku (Kaji Aso International Haiku Competition 2005 HM, 2006 Second Place); Frogpond; The Heron's Nest; kernels; Modern Haiku; Nisqually Delta Review; Notes from the Gean; Now This: Contemporary Poems of Beginnings, Renewals and Firsts; one thing leads to another; Paperclips (HNA 2001 Anthology); Penumbra (Tallahassee Writers' Association Annual Poetry Contest 2006 Finalist, 2007 First Place and Finalist); random moments; The Sacred in Contemporary Haiku; Sidewalk Café; The Temple Bell Stops: Contemporary Poems of Grief, Loss and Change; two poems; Walking the Same Path (HSA 2004 Anthology).

www.ingramcontent.com/pod-product-compliance
Lightning Source LLC
Chambersburg PA
CBHW060049050426
42448CB00011B/2371